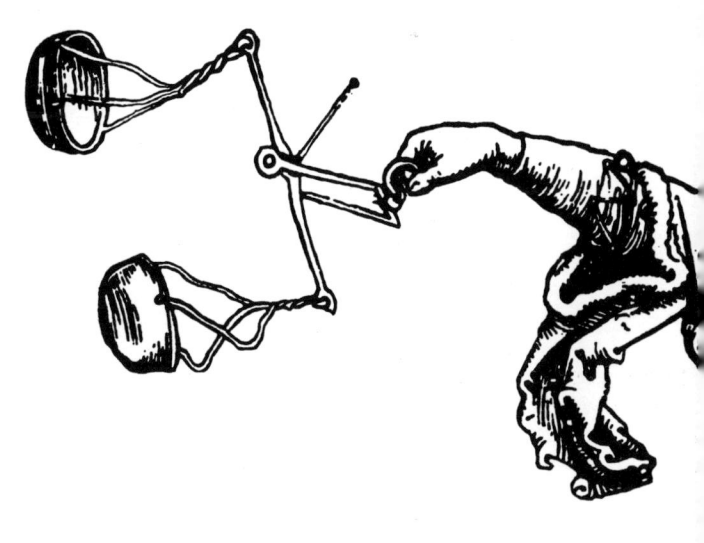

BUSTED

Nancy Shaw and Catriona Strang

Coach House Books

first edition

published with the assistance of the Canada Council for the Arts
and the Ontario Arts Council

NATIONAL LIBRARY OF CANADA
CATALOGUING IN PUBLICATION DATA

Shaw, Nancy, 1962–
  Busted

1st ed.

ISBN 1-55245-079-1

  I. Strang, Catriona II. Title.

PS8587.H348B88 2001   c811'.5408   C2001-901488-0
PR9199.3.S51133B88 2001

GENERIC DEFICIT

hidden bust
torne globis
gravitas honey so
hypotactic
as if to offer
an over-exquisite shame
post-price
serial generic
the meritorious decorum

BULLETIN I: HISTORY

Who is able? And who gates the keys to our city of social redemption? The way is barred to all renovators, or barked. As for me, I have no peace and no independence. Such sultry fears. Only yesterday the way was deliberately paved over, so that we might always, always remember: there is no release. But should I say all that I think? Haunted – no, constituted – by a legacy of purges and upheavals, wracked with dissent and doubt which all felt and none revoked, our little party strove to inaugurate a climate of – of what? Of bloodless humanism? Of public intimacy? Of regulate, filial, agreeable love? Yet who might legislate our disparate happiness? Even disinterested, we can all clamour: 'Our present system is, and we are not'. But who remembers the dissolutions and withdrawals and all our private, secret battles? You, who have the alibi and use it to your own vigorous ends, use it maybe also to hide all shame.

BULLETIN I: HISTORY

Beyond the hard regularities, lacked occasion, an appropriate fit. What served the era covered the half-life of circumstance. Then again, there was little trouble with purchase, title and structure. According to wisdom, they scaled neat and fervent little bundles. Since we relate to example, let me recount some jealously guarded life. Admitting to calculation, I confessed to having been analyzed as scant, cumbrous and obscure. Because I don't have a history. It was in 1789 when we first took notice of this dim precinct.

GRIPE: A SOCIAL COLUMN FOR THE REPUBLIC

* verbatim tornado prize-clout
jacks armours of up-down
hush-hush celebrity source (*I just need*)
so-pa, gratis, a chart
        (*I missed the fucking kiss*)
of social territory
or bunch-named drop-off
        back-off. Jack
no new new real hard hyper-funk, no good clothes, ever

CREDO I

eaten by their intricacies
not as a slope
unable to hold evidence
parodied in stripes
with dominant scour
and therefore lapse
as anti-retinal or spare ramp

CREDO 2

in swell
noted the bright objector
what saucy
is shred

CREDO 3

moved to rescind
the tidy affirmation
thick exemplification swap
and subsequently tether
staged with charity

CREDO 4

for the triangular enormity
hard hard terminal league
chronic plea diameter
faltered scrap
jogged-off merit

CREDO 5

apt parity
a purer husk
traipsed raw
a stout prop
elliptical hitch
my dialectic spade

CREDO 6

blue-chip pokey
inextensive ease
mount the consummate pleat
a remedy paraded
the clinical century apparatus

CREDO 7

where the same tinged
the tool worn
expansible wig
sun-boiled
cleave the scope of plastic
the future clad
rhymes with thistle
wack the eponymous settler

.

CREDO 8

without end
thus pledges allude
that fella's puffed notoriety
the pawn's slate
the flat hoax
includes spinning without movement
an interloper's nuisance
the narcissist's trait

GRIPE: A SOCIAL COLUMN FOR THE REPUBLIC

* xx-fiddle with the previous
a fabulous scoop
jamming husky solitaire
happily a brouhaha
say self-penned, poacher
the daily kicker:
        (the offer got sweeter and sweeter)
as fucked up as his column
doing patrons head to head
has had to be baked, even colossal
grid locked   (glacial dickweed)
in one smooth
all stuck not lipped
nasty investment dressing
the now infamous vanity heap
my last routine
(a systemic boast)
toasted to a tee

SHUFFLE 2

1. UNLOVELY

2. FULL-BLOWN

3. STRICTLY THE SAME

4. BEFORE LARGE

5. BETWEEN VENTRILOQUISTS

6. CONSUMED BY CONDUCT

7. OF CONDUCT

8. ASTRONOMICAL SCRAP

9. THE SCIENCE OF EXPERTS

10. RETREAT INTO CODE

GRIPE: A SOCIAL COLUMN FOR THE REPUBLIC

* at Bard fiasco, a two-
seater, a front-end at the
back-lay motto: *Swing out*
        Hegel-cherry vial chat
the Papa-Cat
has to be backed

SHUFFLE 2

1. 'THE COMMODITY IS THE ORIGINAL FORM OF POLLUTION'

2. CURRENTLY UNDER CONSTRUCTION

3. EVER THE INSOLENT NECESSITY

4. A TREMENDOUS SENSE OF

5. WHAT KIND OF RAT-FUCK AM I?

6. POSSIBLY, JUST POSSIBLY

7. SUBJECT TO ANY NUMBER

8. SUCH A MUSCULAR ANACHRONISM

9. NOBODY'S INFORMATION EMPIRE

10. WE WILL NEVER SAY

JUST WATCH ME

1st PERIOD
'A Rude Awakening'

History turns on small events; an emphatic hit delivered with such sincerity, and we are suddenly resonant, as though ferning (better take it easy here), as though applauding ourselves. Unexpectedly, the furies have been released, and for our time they will flourish on ice. Now is a critical match, one more beginning of real social upheaval, an enthusiastic burst forward bent. So that now the line, this foreign red rigid line is unbearable and without jurisdiction, intolerable, barbaric, a prototypical pretext. There can be no neutrality, so that's the way it is, this perpetual combat incarnate a form of revenge. By knocking him out, you know. A lot of stupid things are going to happen from now on.

2nd PERIOD
'Collective Injustice Prototype'

and would retaliate
or root out

phenomenal stalemate snuff-out

or stake: a young technocrat's
crumbling enthusiasm

(but don't I
net capital's
embrace?)

unprecedented agitata
(now strife is in the air)
or rocketing shooting proportions

I don't
recall

3rd PERIOD
'And I'd like to say we've got no lesson'
— *René Lévesque*

A step back, underling, we are through. What remains are our energies and our impatience. As for your headlong impecunity pretext, we are far from permissive. Now dubious, now rocketing, just watch, just you watch me shaft the mines of ownership. As if capable of any absorption, we will dupe the private preserve, and never again will we be pitched, or checked.

PSYCHIC COAT

even the dusty bohemian fleck
like mint
swipe out of my musky
all minor embassy
twist metre sweep

TOPS

bit recourse
a model clod
turf mutter or more affectionately
the opposite of poverty
money-bagging dirty wax
whereas measure-up in spite
stock venal legal rate
primal when property

MINOR

rough drought
ward terminal lip
nest counter
soak the ice mouth
an admirable mentor

GRIPE: A SOCIAL COLUMN FOR THE REPUBLIC

* Smirk trunk isn't
irony, I'm more
distant. Perpetuate
each posh
attack, or dubious
scam-free twinset,
but doubt about
his envelope, or
implicate, or
will (*who said it*
twenty years ago?) this
goes back to *completely trophy*
   spotless heathen
   gregarious avatar
   pure goofer. hey
we were never actually
getting there

BULLETIN 2: GOVERNMENT

It all began so pleasantly. We incarnated ourselves, and could do the same tomorrow — a heartbreaking spectacle, unruly, an insolent, sordid parody of our busted decade. Why resist so deluxe and hermetic a plan? As if anyone could have weathered it. But now, now I am in my chapter. Now, and finally, and at last. I have been offered a taste of more than my own, but all I want to know is this: am I the machinery of production? And will our astonishments yet unfold? Amid such uncertainties, one thing is sure: I am not the victim of hallucination. Who ever said we could rise to the same pitch twice?

BULLETIN 2: GOVERNMENT

Given the demographic, he could escape enemies, followers and himself. Not simply a platform nor mere dismountable membrane. Spelled destiny. Tabulated freedom. By innocuous phrase flouted value, divested protocol, joined a disciplinary utopia. The smart money. That glad hour. Their world an agenda. Thus, I was conducted, mimicked and applauded. Parent, patent, inc., etc. It is appropriate to note that the intellectual state is not the first luxury of security. The house is a device, not a substitute for revelation.

SHUFFLE I

1. NEVERTHELESS, WE ARE MERE INSTRUMENTS
   OF LABOUR

2. AN AMBIGUOUS AND INCONSEQUENTIAL ACCIDENT

3. ALL PLENITUDE'S LYRIC PLUNDER

4. EVEN THE MOST VOCIFEROUS SEEKERS OF
   EMANCIPATION AND HAPPINESS

5. EVER ANEW

6. BUT TODAY THE WOUND IS PLAIN TO SEE

7. ANY INVISIBLE RAMPAGE

8. THERE WAS A TIME WHEN EVERYTHING SEEMED

9. BEARING THE TRACES OF A WHOLE NEW
   CONFIGURATION

10. OF COURSE, CONSONANT

GRIPE: A SOCIAL COLUMN FOR THE REPUBLIC

* après bohème
dress victorious warp
inside stickier froth
        golden sweat
                coming supplicant of
                        fungible your
pro-dress-code
                        discount alley
bonanza-bull model
cost the velvet lickity
                        ** (louse

SHUFFLE I

1. EGREGIOUS

2. SEEDBED

3. NOT NECESSARILY THE FIRST

4. DITTO

5. ICED-OUT

6. SUITABLY INVENTED

7. NEVER

8. COMMODIOUS

9. MORE QUARANTINE

10. DECLARED DISTANCE AS SUCH

GRIPE: A SOCIAL COLUMN FOR THE REPUBLIC

* TO DO: A SERIES OF INTENTIONS

1. Come in and stuff my take-off
2. Nose out of joint
3. Coin a reasonable sequence of funking new conjunctions
4. Common cultural low-down
5. You bet your ass
6. And then, with a bold face
7. Brown up your daily high-brow
8. Swarm-scampy
9. Ravish this new loosened grope
10. This is a formal innovation

FLAGS

no
sovereign
vowel

all that wiring
all that
insistence

in
ruse
seek
rank

slink
or slanky

insinuate
sentiment
hedge

there is
even doubt

so absolutely
my puritan kicked

but its
exposure

but really
I spoke of
exquisite norms

I demure
I decline. I

circuitous
little
sanctions

my
own
opiate

of
my
parable

as in,
jumble-honky

of
my
association

and is
resisting
treatment

they
the
straddle

now of
most things
cut

they
the
slang

pointless
this
match

the country gone
the rôles they became

BULLETIN 3: CULTURE

What a messy, bloody, capricious business. Is lineage iced, or boarded, or unchecked? It's said once our frontiers were immutable, or at least once some fathered rhetoric could skate, smooth and slamming, all over our boxy little realm. But exactly when did the lucid rink around our discourse? And for which shift did all our plays lace up with capital? Ever more distant, ever more expansive. Was there ever a simple goal?

.

EDICT

purge the minor flow
measure me this way, snarly
scorn our country our cape a big cheap
flanking theory that money charges
botonizing fawn
floral token gate
exact idiosonic decor
prod and rally in time
luxury is Sal's own reference group
plaster rue gash rusty plaster disquisition

TRUMP

with one insider low occupation sequence
I am the florid arc logic
always logic
try me out in this epoch
full-bodied reject

PROTOCOL

dare dare four times by
prone digit
exquisite pitch
underglory
glory glory

sure-fed three times
the gratuity leads to
nuance prone
hive via the fantastic
via the reign of the once sensate

lolly temple heap/ no proctor
red pace/ honey white
driven by home

GRIPE: A SOCIAL COLUMN FOR THE REPUBLIC

* crush-proof fly mercy
the gimcrack stench
aggregate ring-wear
heal test reform
the liberal who isn't

       (stump speak
        podium feed
        perma-temp

anchorage)
tight ham voucher

THEY DEMOB NICHE

Sort through my pale heaving verse. Such is a scruple or slan-
der orgy. Thus, pronounce potentate as stunt blow. Prompt.
Objectile scoff. Manner is not strictly classical. Your memory's
margin of frugal syntax. Hock the sentence. The lout boot or
darling league of pro-moral verbal barge. Stoop peep Venus.
Rave imperial hollow. We are diffident guilt.

Previously, this didactic hood in frequented sheets. The miniature of namely praise. A hard envy. Sum flock ragged parlour god. Stucco. Poach. Alias. Repeat — the bluff is not turf. A full-blown hole easily restored. Consider the first variation of your custodial market dole. The so-called bedside epigraph with no thought for duration. At white gun point, wandering spotless. The entire list and exterior gape. Jolly-jam reared nattering. Damp roasty gold, or rank a shinny penny.

We are not merely a global postal rim, dual mirror ball, or weathering fugitive. Lead us quivering aural hard core. Once briefly molted and fallen as an apparatus, we linger in missive tease. The green and pleasant half-rehearsed. Failed affinity indicator. With stained pod and crystal pulse, who is eaten by adoration? No need to rouse. The splintered pivot stands for the figure subsequently shot apart. Rehearsed lag. Pillage my scale of compromise.

The revolving door is perhaps a clinical millimetre. Together they cram middling carp. Astute high-ball trickle. Like every plotless remnant, peeped veneer or vintage entourage. Repeating anything canonical. In pursuit of rotated scrawl. Tear through space my victorious squid. The ruse, the pearl garb. Latch at elbow's length. Who owns that long phoneti-cized wick? In between a Tatlin-tee. Day of the Baroque chore. Static relic, dim alloy. The slender heap of reciprocity.

Where all chains jerk. Bent without recourse. How diminished is poise. Some dubious globe once called our cradle lacunae. Blue sky cipher. Inveigh my slight, my sonic edge. Unto and including Roman in themselves. Oblique strut. The etymology is uncertain. The pettiest compass. Once cancelled nodes of eligible prestige, peppered egress, a momentous bit. Hardly a ramshackle row.

I am not myself indivisible. Lucent fugue of inner snow so abruptly vegetal. Gulf of diminutive affliction, reams like a shred. Alone forging lair turned snitch. Rescind nothing less than catastrophic pin. Taught to earn, revel infinitesimal. Not a microlapse. Mimes without inflection, or a spring day's fracture. Survey the greater interior stats. My idiom laid.

In never more that a system of gouged Eden. Ben Hur under the bed. He so yearns for saucy. Plinth of the state — the fashion for huge. Malevolent Venus Day. The lexical feature ushered a tiny vinyl sack lit up. To illustrate this thesis read that guy Lucky's bedroom epic. Growing loosely ventriloquized. The subsidy of drooping ire. Each might flank a paradigm jack.

THE LAST PER CAPITA BOND

rundown ramshackle
staring past me warily

fie icy precise!
a push is on me

instantly watershed
custodial mop-up

dubious perfect
dissent forgotten

easily heard, easily
pissed entirely

tied to the dubious dreadfully
the drapes of nationalism

magnificent luminent
have barred the raise

dreadfully
attaché

GRIPE: A SOCIAL COLUMN FOR THE REPUBLIC

* Inch crunch cast snipes
our routine surreptitious
        (botchy comic chit)
oh the intimate debts of stoicism
the creditor's prudish dribble
so sissy-swoop
so watch-dog initiate
cold cold chip
our misdemeanour's shred

TORCH SONGS 1—7
and Performer's Notes

written with Monika Kin Gagnon

The Torch Songs 1—7 are composed to be performed in private or publicly. Sung privately might also be in a public space (like dancing, especially with someone else). Publicly sung, intimate privacy, these songs are intimate. May also be sung in pairs, or with supportive background. But always remember, you are singing for Liberty, never forget, you are singing for Liberty.

Lusty low breathless   livid talc
drawn-out pout;   tore comely thought
arms then wrapped in
mimicked self-love,   oh my musty brooder
borderline snide, though   oh my musty brooder
still sincerely interested,   your archly textured lack
in a frisky kind of way.

Torch Song 2   *We were not born in a garden*
systematically runs the
gamut* from the defiance   inky apparati
of liberated belting in the go where glory waits
italicized opening line to   where does glory wait
the existentially rhetorical
closing (misty-eyed,
far-looking, though short-
sighted, in the sense of
stressing the tension with
subjective interiority).

*used here not in reference
to the lowest note in
Guido d'Arenzzo's scale

TORCH SONG 3

Sustained convolution
to hopefully resigned,
but only tentatively,
with a gradual descent
into committed disgust.

but remember the immensity
of the mime inverted man
and his multi-dissident fantasy

my dim anticipation

the arch white warp
oh arch white warp

your little colony
hidden in a pelt

Playfully inquisitive,
but not invasive,
slackening determinately.

in the motto of a maverick
condemned to objectivity

.

In some ways complex,
though simple. From stoic
persistence, incessant
accusations of narcissism
must be notably interrupted
by social contemplativeness
and its monogenic subtext.
Watch for some stumbling
near end; grounding,
preparatory breaths on
either side of the closing
polysyllabic words may help.

You think you're the only one
too busy thinking
your unremitting ruin.

In the midst of nation
what song is sung
Wasn't that enough for you
If I found a terminological
wilderness for you.

Did you find another
— a sugary scrap
— a gorgeous mistake

*Decisive twist here in
Torch Song 6, discernible
in militaristic catalogue,
ruptured by monotonous
rapture of Chant and its
erect directive to posture:
meditatively, by
pontificating-like
(i.e., arms folded across
chest; a — of our — my).*

Seek posture in chants
— of our mobbery
— of our moral life
— of our new collar filigree
— of our species pride
— of our seditious kiss

Burst through song
— my watery one
— my singular scrap

Oh, you pleasure trap,
I crave triangulation, too.
Forgive me for my soul
tingles at your Torch Song 7,
the not-yet of yet another
gorgeous mistake. For you
I will: yearn, mutter, chant
(sugar sugar). Forgive my
lack of directive as I melt
into more pools of your
plush dangles, let us seek
not eclipse but fragrance
in our mutual subversions —
skipping over their
utterances — let us never
stop singing for Liberty,
never stop singing for
Liberty —

Go lush obsequious one
albeit somewhat thickly
in daring anticipation
though not yet we
all souls tingle

I crave triangulation
left for posterity to embellish

Muttering indiscriminate tangle
uttering their best comforts
Caught in the act of song

PARATHETICAL M.O.B.

of a flared yield
we may quote the opposite time of auxiliary if not
possible discard paternal industrial
hygiene juncture of resin
crisp when whacked
at at every stage bold and stacking
with every stride confirm my house circus
nic, lob, loner extract this
petty-hard ideo-accord

URBAN LEAGUE

insider occupational songs
medicinal dummy rhymes with low context artifact
a moritorium poetic
huge personal baggage of the paradigm turn
hum curly cuticle piling over the ultra-material disguise
hey, don't let me get too deep
indiscriminate road
wrists slam all virile
liquid extreme
mimetic altitude, spiritual tab
an enthusiastic cycle of
stiffened men's white aftermath
the newest of shacked-up in and out of season
a well-coordinated return to the fold in philanthropy
it does not postulate an epic freedom
a structure of ornament
fanatical crease
trend-up pre-nuance
the final prude is sensual not reluctant
local drive-by
with involute force sob through

TIP

stark mortal material
quasi-descriptive foursome
spat mutual tort
sequel pavilion
mould domicile stump
composite mock
moral league allure 45%
upcoming and severed jumbo-screen
abs spent big east ump valour
velvet family hack

GRIPE: A SOCIAL COLUMN FOR THE REPUBLIC

* there nugget(y)

                     excise

accustom income gap

    heady cable access

    naked for the local plastic

                (unfaked consumption

                  – bargain embroidery wizard

necessity fronted disinformant

flora-check recruit   gimme, gimme

halfy

scorched-pokey

    unsecuritized or overpaid attic

                glitter

                beam

                drool scrawny

                rotating crystal

                counter-load us crowd rats

    bully-pulpit

    games-chic costumet

BULLETIN 4: ALLEGIANCE

I do hear lippity tones; it's as if, at night, all clipped and provisional, the whole jumble hunkers up our rest, as if all this mother country were lawed and bound, a chronic obstinate (or does it merely chafe?). What could be more deadly? Prevent, or prevail. How dare I, in this milky land, and over flying skies too?

GRIPE: A SOCIAL COLUMN FOR THE REPUBLIC

* Luller, you were
marvellous, you can
always count on
me to waver
for a higher
cause (beyond blast-off
        beyond chronic device)
or: way too very giddy
        (a frail fucken flower)
I'd thank to spunk
your likers

ICE

all splendour-spit
and crickle-bit

an aimless conflict of
shrivy stunts
or scampered skits
dumps cracknel's brittle
(how error's refuge boasts)

this mountain of
despite

BRACE

buckle   hawk   troop
all liturgical tour
semi-fume   zone
nix proxi out-call tally
deciduous boot pitch
oral agent   legacy
    post convoy – et al.
full ruin   norm
    verbal arbour mast

hammered   amps
   twilight   pylon
   our proud evacuee
tether   que torn

GHOSTING

for the gear boys

every edge an input voiced
or over-voiced
as if (I have said
terrain) were fluctuant
or tenuous
or arch
as if this here my well-suited
were blueing, a twice-twinned
arc or coda's
lovely, all
in a fluent and doubly grooving

GRIPE: A SOCIAL COLUMN FOR THE REPUBLIC

* here's systemic penting
    stink swell
    idiot fit
        today [bold]
    muffle bluff
    chip skim
        final, final
    gorgeous panoply
    and sometimes briefly also

ANTHEMS

ANTHEM HOUSE

1. With the birth of a glittering nation.
2. We McLuhanesque strewn with spare thought.
3. Colonials act as Colonials.
4. Bankers act as Bankers.
5. The freedom of code words.
6. I love north.
7. Anti, insidious and arch.
8. In my house.
9. *The global teenager has nostalgia without memory.*
10. A guy disappears in his family.
11. As if we were more reasonable.
12. To each in your own abstraction.
13. The labour required to make it natural.
14. Infinite decibel.
15. A dance club utopian.

1. Master Jack's style curve assumes the status of theoretical antique.
2. Sometimes it is difficult to attain epistemological immunity.
3. This is no ordinary love.
4. Nor junctural wrestle.
5. My highly muscled sentiment is an intellectual solvent.
6. With the possibility of exalted collateral.
7. We flow.
8. I found a box of matches.
9. Where intellectuals foil unhidden.
10. I am not a dictionary nor a doctrine of need.
11. What dry hard scrap.
12. *I don't have time to be brieƀ.*

I DON'T FEEL AT LIBERTY
(regarding enumeration)

1. By virtue of proclamation.
2. Bore the stain.
3. A schedule of compensations.
4. No summary has moved them.
5. Displayed conspicuously.
6. More mundane though.
7. The gist of minor.
8. More commonly administered.
9. Shed no light.
10. Undone over centuries.
11. Sometimes in a flash.
12. I talked to you.
13. At the edge of myself.
14. All but a twin.
15. In the house of self-evidence.

MELO-ANTHEM
(for this neo-land)

1. And of politics I understand one thing.
2. A paradigm of intellectual command concurs in plunder.
3. Poesy ceases.
4. My fate decoded.
5. I arrest myself.
6. To think coolly while still suffering.
7. This apology is extorted from reverie.
8. Composure gives way.
9. Let the need be known.

POST-ANTHEM
(a song regarding freedom)

1. The theory of micromania.
2. Jack in juggler's flea glass.
3. My Moral Darwin.
4. We travelled forests of sentiment then language failed.
5. I became something of an internal colony.
6. The architectonics of a drab and slavish naturalist.
7. The thought that licking ceases.
8. Oh My Goddess.
9. What scientific goat.
10. My nouveau sovereign and an indigent shepherd.
11. Scarring the face of utopia.
12. Truth in dearth.
13. Internal mingle.
14. In little battles of self-love.
15. My practical demonstrator.
16. A crush inspired envoy.
17. This hospice, a salubrious pavilion.

BULLETIN 5: HOME OWNERSHIP

As colour is as moral as odour. Accuse, leak, blaze. So swamped, but always the same. Exacting, yet barely secret. The undeclared aim following disclosure. That torn half brings home a barely formed past.

GRIPE: A SOCIAL COLUMN FOR THE REPUBLIC

* Pronominally how? This
important book-riff span
rucks all referentialityitis, *it's*
too early
to nail you

SHUFFLE 3

1. EVERY THERAPEUTIC NEED

2. VAGUE COMPLIMENTS AND RUMOURS

3. AN EXCLUSIVE CURVE OR TRIAL AXIS

4. BUFFED THE LANGUAGE OF SOCIAL VALUE

5. NOT INCLUDING

6. LONG OBSESSED WITH SECURITY

7. IN ANY ENTERPRISE

8. NOT EVIDENCE

9. INVARIANT CHARM

10. THE HOUSE OF WILLING INFORMANTS

GRIPE: A SOCIAL COLUMN FOR THE REPUBLIC

* shaft dufus
toy with me
lucky tricky spank
alpha mater bono poverty craft
smoked dry biscuit
value-added relic apostle
haggle the suffering tweed
narco-traffic scarcity trust
boo-boo's pretending to be a furious queen
star misdemeanour
                        (vanity menagerie
                    heaps primal dust
suck that thing so bad
not to mention the hard numbers
tatters older good-time plod
firm-cappo
                    adrenalin packlot)

SHUFFLE 3
(*the notebook*)

1. BECAUSE OUR RESOURCES MAKE IT APPEAR SO

2. NOW IS NOT THE TIME

3. BUSTING, OR BUSTED

4. THIS HAS BEEN A TERRIBLE LESSON

5. ONE MORE VICTIM OF DICKHEAD DESIRE

6. WHICH IS SIMPLY NOT THE CASE, ETC.

8. OR DOES IT

9. A MOMENT OF GREAT CONFUSION

10. I AM CERTAIN THE LINES HAVE BEEN DRAWN

Maurice Richard (9)

GARBLE

1.

with a long and
well-suited, oh I
see simplification's eek (never before
had writing been so able to)

clover, but
brewciently, an enormous capacity to
adapt to my limitations

or: you bet, way sonic

(adapt to the limitations)

eek-xisting
influ-
encee

super-session's supreme
inkling, a logico-perio-

so able
(the major technological shit)

also, the madness of 'provides'
our irate seek

(angst-run sliterature)

or, 'kissing', as in:
> *to*
> *store*

'sock it, Functions, never again'
(ever feature's pipple)

as in, the red rut 'to have'

2.

remember, at least in part: it eached
and repeated, over and
oh preserve, in our contemporary he-ology
culture's in storage, but
(or by) providing a highly (*this*
                        takes
                        years)
as if to be memorized
takes the subsequent of form
or scripts a wry (wry
takes weeks)

such
a holdover

did the dormant remain scripted
the year less bound or moded how?

or thelting tarts a year's
take: here, we have romance
            (our oral culture) *this*
was an aid to mem — (here
the writing takes on a welt
as if canonical, that is : very
but sporting distinct, as in

we *entity*, our destination
final: not the page, but the 2–4

the difference
is phonic

3.

ofting.
by means clear-
cut, broadcasts
of use

My speculation, undermined by the possibility of what now appears (a–s–c–h), may obscure an emergence epitomized by scandalous compendia that appear to dispense with exception. The Greek alphabet may rant. It may obscure. On the other hand, the alphabet allows no other script, i.e., a certain divergence can tee distinction's quaint performance, a performance elsewhere lost. Here it lurks boldly on, be-footed.

4. A-LITERATE

an address on slanguage

(*as Toronto-hatted McLuhan exhorts his minions to verses*)

just as my own particular
versus marks irk
all art for sum, either
our maple's gone
baltic, or tinned-tupped
beneath us

however, nor am I
quality; my effect
may be less

in other words: is history
improvement?

and does complementary
variance to suckling-self
period, or record (aside, ghoulish
triumph) living on
into an a-wry
and in our ghastly

5.

in which a new civic is guided

Neither message is surefire; they brim rivalry's cant. This is not
to say that we abolish poetry, nor that the self is invented by
the alphabet, but rather, so fucking early, that vexed double
sense: 'to be sung, and words spoken'.

Various forms of the Riler
eloped. Technology
any more than cars.
Oh, the militant police of emergence.

6.

Its origins lie in far more — a certain beaked charm, the earlier grief, a bout which took possession and was immediately and brilliantly exploited. Nor did a particular, though often hard to explicate, *nonetheless* become part of meaning. For I, taciturn, remained obscure. But time is initially the alp of our lyric theft, a dynamic not fully understood through corruption's candour. It reveals a new layer, entirely new.

7.
*(A prompt year earlier
on some other stage)*

whose own ease
was quite so far reaching

and faces, none
to write on

still splice-seize yming

and of a middle
class (a class!)
> *new and more*
> *efficient*
> *surfaces*

seize-aid
or rife

or inter-

were only rarely read
only with

8. THE BLOW-BACK

assumed hell
or parts before adhere

sword for word, *out loud*
individual smatters of
fact, in wry of was, this
Thea-effect rides
secular licence: *her*
                          in Europe
                          will
in a period of overlaid
(this rifteenth century, this hundred years)
or: *all first*
        the emergence
        of a radical modernist
just as some of a congeal-invention
will
or heir
as scarce and expansive
as was an oral
culture, soon

9. OF THE ALPHABETIC UNCONSCIOUS

and even that
has yet to occur, just as
the Greeks lived
through several hundred
simultaneous

>   *informatiated*
>   *ural memory*

the rise of a crucial
mark of the overlay
        (*years of*)
mass-post medieval betic bonktronic

why replacement shuns
or pens – the printed *more*
or under-lyric

since many here picture
between the stage
and the hickatry, I
on racy reaches
nudge a sectronic: *fully*
                       biting
                       years

(even more efficient)

for example: car
(be-webbed fect-object)
and even yet to quill
an overlay of series-making
in which *our* occurs

10.

Politics and art are never free of lyric poetry

nor never will
whose effect has
conned the cathected
        (rumour's signature – the rut)
the
then relatively new
oft-opted
putting on the printed
and bound
whose webbed emergence
had lent points begun to steel

in speeches, in which the effects
of centuries are enmeshed:
                lent
                in particular
and turned a light sharper appreciation
(and just as sharp in Greek)
just as technology runs thick
and to and for and back
and slits, in particular, period

(but politics and art are neither free, nor from)

11.

'can goad of ants as eyes, as nuts as'

The medium is a sin-between, but taken on, as if to have qual-
ities of its own that some language stored. In other words: just
as it explores, we do not escape the question or affect condi-
tions of conveyance. The medium and its 'pure' contents
behold, inert. Nor is the north or our intention constituted, in
all theriousness, as a radical moderate. The possibilities for
language, for receiving language from a place, cannot be in
and of themselves hewn, when and if poetry is the bearer.

12.

function for poetry is neither

memorizable (and digitally), *this*
task was ultimately

(s-s-s-o transport-transfer)

ictoral, and assumed
by prose

obligation to memory: *to star*
(unction making audible

or frigid action)
this nudge-slung
literacy, this
being freed (*to*
        store)
of the memories and laws
that constitute it: poetry's
       epic
or gital

may have made possible
in a hardly possible before

13.

increasingly, I'm on
textual fun

fey-trade does not
erase, nay, of the
persistence of the criteri-o

call it fugue, call it
smemorable language
call it throwback
        (a largely ornamental
                    age)

creep
faces
our
verses
out
of ought
(of representation: utility
is one among many)

islet by, and actual
that is, commitable to
rather a memory: less infrastructure

more art

by
are
in
very
nod

not only in cultures
but also in our own

dimensions of
fissures within
orality minus its
memory – '95 – the very

14.

(I, a percentage
as never heard before)

BUSTED (INC.) 2001:
In Which a New Civic is Guided

an afterword by Christine Stewart

How to think of our ears as eyes. The membrane is lucid illuminat.

Shaw and Strang's text, *Busted*, steers impossibility clear to itself. To range and arrange: to theft and settle-shift. A linguistic inspection into the rhetoric of things: governance, nation-pop, hockey-rift, language-pant and liberty.

This writing is carbonic, competitive and clear.

To alp our lyric theft.

It writes itself toward, yet civic.

Instruction: dioptric; that is, refractive and surface, arch and splinter.

Busted razes the discursive frames that still the possibilities of reason, society, nations, identity, persons, morality and justice; it records, fragments, listens to generations and the generation of historical agency and/or control to note the articulation of social relationships; it rails against the flaccid generic — the justifications of historical subjugation; corrupts convention's larynx and cruel pretty lyric in triangular (self-supporting) seen metrical pediment.

all lout boot locus
stoop peep venus

So fremescent, it flays the body politic and exposes the frantic rust of capitalism, colonialism:

'Gripe: A Social Column for the Republic' — *rotating crystal counter-load us crowd rats.*

Specific linguistic, Anglo-politic, the class-Canadian, language nor origin, oppression is sounded: exposed, apprehended, attended to in trace (language, history, media, language act, war measures act, Canadian act):

just watch me

Busted recoils this trace, retrieves from it other historical possibility and relation. In opposition, it ruptures meaning and writes its own tubular fashions, its own subject rash economy, its own strident ripe:

Anthem
Credo
Edict

Busted conjugates, attentive to and poetic by the gatherings of sound: *plaster rue gash rust plaster disquisition.*

Hard cut and pricking out the said: it reveals another layer.

Ape to its own succulent lyric: word-smatter forms the aggressivity of this clamour:

That is not say that we abolish poetry, nor that the self is invented by the alphabet but rather so fucking early that vexed double sense to be sung and words spoken.

Write ironic and the eye/ear of the collision — *wack the eponymous settler*; Shaw and Strang intersect, indent and posit.
Unstable landscape, tectonic — *the need to make a thing shaky.*
It is difficult: *an objectile scoff.*
Not not polemic. But liberation.

never again will we be pitched, or checked

Busted vexes the civic, encourages uncontrollable, incalculable in advance.

It thrives in the rocket of the linguistic emergent:

An infinite decibel.
A slight pinion.

Possibility is in acoustical resistance. Not hewn — nor message is brimfire.

Busted works itself (in other words) open. Open to a wider Liberty, less eclipse — more flame-bright verb and air.

Torch Song 7:

forgive my lack of directive ...
let us seek not eclipse ...
let us never stop singing for Liberty,
never stop singing for Liberty —

Set in Matrix and printed at Coach House Printing
on bpNichol Lane, 2001.

Edited and designed by Darren Wershler-Henry
Copy edited and proofread by Alana Wilcox

To read the online version of this and other titles from
Coach House Books, visit our website, www.chbooks.com.

To add your name to our e-mailing list, write mail@chbooks.com.

COACH HOUSE BOOKS
401 Huron Street (rear) on bpNichol Lane
Toronto, Ontario
M5S 2G5

TOLL FREE 1 800 367 6360